IT

DO WE LIVE IN A SIMULATION?

CONTENTS

Introduction

The Simulation Hypothesis proposes that our perceived reality is, in fact, a computer-generated simulation created by a more advanced civilization. The idea has gained traction in recent years, with prominent figures like Elon Musk and Neil deGrasse Tyson publicly discussing the possibility that we are living in a simulated reality.

The concept of a simulated reality has deep roots in philosophical thought, with Plato's "Allegory of the Cave" and René Descartes' "Evil Demon" arguments providing early examples of similar ideas. However, the recent advancement of technology and the exponential growth of computing power have led to a resurgence of interest in the Simulation Hypothesis.

This book will explore the Simulation Hypothesis in depth, examining the philosophical, scientific, and cultural implications of the theory. We will explore the arguments for and against a simulated reality, the role of technology in shaping our understanding of reality, and the potential impact of a simulated reality on humanity's future. Join us on this journey as we delve into the fascinating world of the Simulation Hypothesis and attempt to answer one of the most profound questions of our time: *Do we live in a simulation?*

What is really reality?
The world you see or the world you don't see?
Or both?
The perception of your reality might not be at all what it seems to be...

CHAPTER 1

The Historical Roots of the Simulation Hypothesis

The Simulation Hypothesis has a long and complex history, with roots stretching back thousands of years. While the concept of a simulated reality has been discussed in various forms throughout history, the modern version of the Simulation Hypothesis emerged in the late 20th century.

One of the earliest examples of the Simulation Hypothesis can be found in Plato's "Allegory of the Cave," in which he describes a group of people who have spent their entire lives chained in a cave, only able to see shadows on the wall. The allegory suggests that our understanding of reality is limited by our perception and that there may be a deeper reality beyond what we can perceive.

Another early example can be found in René Descartes' "Evil Demon" argument, in which he proposes that an evil demon may be deceiving us into believing in a false reality. This argument served as a precursor to the modern Simulation Hypothesis by suggesting that our perceptions may be misleading, and that reality may not be as it appears.

In the mid-20th century, science fiction began to explore the idea of simulated realities, with works like Philip K. Dick's "Ubik" and Stanisław Lem's "The Futurological Congress" exploring the concept. In the 1980s, the computer revolution gave rise to a new wave of interest in the Simulation Hypothesis, with computer scientists and philosophers beginning to seriously consider the possibility that our reality could be a simulation.

The modern version of the Simulation Hypothesis was popularized by philosopher Nick Bostrom in his 2003 paper "Are You Living in a Computer Simulation?" Bostrom proposed that it is not only possible but likely that we are living in a simulation created by a more advanced civilization.

Today, the Simulation Hypothesis continues to be a subject of intense debate and speculation, with scientists, philosophers, and the general public all weighing in on the possibility that our reality is not as it seems.

CHAPTER 2
The Philosophical Case for a Simulated Reality

The Philosophical Case for a Simulated Reality is based on the idea that our reality may not be as it appears, and that it could be a product of an advanced civilization's computer simulation. This argument is grounded in several philosophical principles and thought experiments that suggest that the nature of reality is not fixed, and that our perceptions may not be a reliable guide to what is truly real.

One such thought experiment is the "Brain in a Vat" scenario, which suggests that a brain could be kept alive in a vat of nutrients and connected to a computer that simulates reality. In this scenario, the brain would have no way of distinguishing between the simulation and the real world, leading to the conclusion that our perceptions may not be a reliable guide to what is real.

Another thought experiment that supports the Philosophical Case for a Simulated Reality is the "Simulation Argument," which proposes that if it is possible to create a simulated reality that is indistinguishable from the real world, it is likely that advanced civilizations have already done so. If this is the case, the argument suggests that it is more likely that we are living in a simulation than in the real world.

The Philosophical Case for a Simulated Reality also draws on the concept of a "multiverse," which suggests that there may be an infinite number of parallel universes, each with its own unique version of reality. If this is true, it is possible that our reality is just one of many simulations that have been created by advanced civilizations in other universes.

Ultimately, the Philosophical Case for a Simulated Reality challenges our assumptions about the nature of reality and the limits of human knowledge. It suggests that our perceptions may not be a reliable guide to what is real, and that the only way to know for sure if we are living in a simulation is to uncover evidence that supports or refutes the Simulation Hypothesis.

CHAPTER 3
The Scientific Case for a Simulated Reality

The Scientific Case for a Simulated Reality is based on the idea that the universe behaves in a way that is consistent with a computer simulation. This argument draws on several scientific principles and observations that suggest that our reality may be a product of an advanced civilization's computer simulation.

One such principle is the idea of the universe as a mathematical structure. Many scientists believe that the universe can be described using mathematical equations and that these equations could be run on a computer to simulate reality. This suggests that our universe may be a product of a simulation rather than a physical, objective reality.

Another principle that supports the Scientific Case for a Simulated Reality is the concept of quantum mechanics. The behaviour of subatomic particles is often unpredictable and seems to be affected by observation, leading some scientists to suggest that reality is shaped by our perceptions of it. This idea is consistent with the idea that our reality is a product of a computer simulation, in which the simulation's programmers' control what we perceive as reality.

Additionally, some scientists have proposed that the universe exhibits features that are consistent with a simulated reality. For example, in 2003, physicist James Gates discovered that certain equations that describe fundamental particles appear to contain computer code similar to that used in computer simulations. This discovery suggests that the universe may be a product of a computer simulation.

The Scientific Case for a Simulated Reality also draws on the concept of the holographic principle, which suggests that the universe may be a 3D projection of information stored on a 2D surface. This idea is consistent with the idea that the universe is a product of a computer simulation, in which the simulation's programmers could use a 2D surface to store information about our 3D reality.

While the Scientific Case for a Simulated Reality is still a subject of debate among scientists, the idea that our reality may be a product of a computer simulation is a fascinating and thought-provoking concept that challenges our understanding of the nature of reality.

CHAPTER 4
The Religious Implications of a Simulated Reality

The Religious Implications of a Simulated Reality are complex and far-reaching, challenging traditional beliefs about the nature of God, the afterlife, and the meaning of existence. The idea that our reality may be a product of an advanced civilization's computer simulation raises important questions about the role of religion in understanding the universe and our place in it.

One of the most significant religious implications of a simulated reality is the challenge it poses to the idea of a creator God. If our reality is a product of a computer simulation created by an advanced civilization, it is difficult to reconcile this with the idea of a creator God who is responsible for creating the universe. This raises questions about the nature of God, and whether the concept of a creator is relevant in a simulated reality.

The idea of an afterlife is also challenged by the concept of a simulated reality. Many religions suggest that our consciousness survives after death and moves on to another realm, but in a simulated reality, our consciousness would be a product of a computer program, making it unlikely that it could survive beyond the termination of the program. This raises questions about the meaning of existence and the purpose of life, and challenges traditional beliefs about the nature of the soul and the afterlife.

Additionally, the idea of a simulated reality raises questions about the concept of free will. If our reality is a product of a computer program, it is possible that our actions and decisions are predetermined by the program's code. This challenges the idea of free will, which is a fundamental concept in many religions.

Overall, the Religious Implications of a Simulated Reality challenge traditional religious beliefs and raise important questions about the nature of God, the afterlife, and the meaning of existence. The idea that our reality may be a product of a computer simulation challenges our assumptions about the universe and challenges us to re-examine our beliefs in light of new scientific and philosophical discoveries.

CHAPTER 5
The Ethics of Creating and Living in a
Simulated Reality

The Ethics of Creating and Living in a Simulated
Reality are complex and thought-provoking. If we
are living in a simulated reality or have the ability to
create one, it raises important ethical questions
about our responsibilities to the simulated beings
within the simulation and the potential
consequences of our actions.

One of the primary ethical questions raised by the
idea of a simulated reality is whether it is ethical to
create sentient beings within the simulation. If the
beings within the simulation are capable of
experiencing pain and pleasure, it raises questions
about whether it is ethical to create them and
subject them to suffering.

Another ethical question is the potential
consequences of creating and living in a simulated
reality. If our reality is a simulation, it is possible
that our actions could have unintended
consequences on the simulated beings within the
simulation. This raises questions about our

responsibilities to those beings and whether we should consider their well-being when making decisions that could impact their lives.

The creation and living in a simulated reality also raise questions about the concept of consent. If the beings within the simulation are sentient, it raises questions about whether it is ethical to create them without their consent or to manipulate their experiences within the simulation without their knowledge.

Additionally, the creation and living in a simulated reality raises questions about the nature of reality and whether it is ethical to choose to live in a simulated reality rather than the physical world. This raises questions about the value of physical experience and the potential consequences of choosing to live in a simulated reality.

Overall, the Ethics of Creating and Living in a Simulated Reality are complex and raise important questions about our responsibilities to the beings within the simulation and the potential consequences of our actions. It challenges us to consider the ethical implications of our choices and to question the nature of reality and our place within it.

CHAPTER 6

The Limits of Human Knowledge and Perception

The Limits of Human Knowledge and Perception are important considerations in exploring the possibility of a simulated reality. Our ability to understand and perceive the world around us is limited by our cognitive abilities, sensory perception, and the tools we use to explore the world. This raises important questions about whether we can ever truly know whether our reality is a simulation or not.

One of the primary limits of human knowledge and perception is our reliance on our senses. Our senses provide us with information about the world around us, but they can also be deceived or limited in their ability to perceive certain aspects of reality. For example, our eyes can only perceive a small portion of the electromagnetic spectrum, meaning that there may be aspects of reality that we are unable to perceive.

Another limit to human knowledge and perception is our cognitive abilities. Our ability to reason, understand complex concepts, and think abstractly is limited by our biological makeup and the structure of our brains. This raises questions about whether we are capable of understanding a reality that may be vastly different from our own.

Additionally, the tools we use to explore the world can also limit our knowledge and perception. For example, scientific instruments are designed to measure specific aspects of reality and may not be capable of detecting aspects of reality that fall outside their scope.

Ultimately, the Limits of Human Knowledge and Perception suggest that there may be aspects of reality that are beyond our understanding and perception. This raises important questions about whether we can ever truly know whether our reality is a simulation or not, and whether the concept of a simulated reality is even comprehensible to human beings. Despite these limitations, however, exploring the possibility of a simulated reality challenges us to question our assumptions about the nature of reality and our place within it.

CHAPTER 7
The Nature of Consciousness in a Simulated Reality

The Nature of Consciousness in a Simulated Reality is an important consideration when exploring the possibility that our reality is a computer-generated simulation. If our reality is a simulation, it raises questions about whether consciousness is a product of the simulation or whether it exists independently of the simulation.

One possible explanation for consciousness in a simulated reality is that it is a product of the simulation's programming. In this scenario, consciousness would be an emergent property of the simulation, similar to the way that the behavior of a colony of ants emerges from the interactions of individual ants. This would suggest that consciousness is not an independent phenomenon but rather a product of the simulation itself.

Another possible explanation for consciousness in a simulated reality is that it exists independently of the simulation. In this scenario, consciousness would be a fundamental aspect of reality that exists outside of the simulation and is not dependent on the simulation for its existence. This would suggest that consciousness is a product of the physical world rather than a product of the simulation.

Additionally, the nature of consciousness in a simulated reality raises questions about the nature of subjective experience. If consciousness is a product of the simulation, it raises questions about whether subjective experience is real or simply an illusion created by the simulation. Alternatively, if consciousness exists independently of the simulation, it suggests that subjective experience is a fundamental aspect of reality that cannot be reduced to the workings of a computer program.

Overall, the Nature of Consciousness in a Simulated Reality is a complex and thought-provoking topic that challenges our assumptions about the nature of consciousness and its relationship to the physical world. It raises important questions about the limits of computer simulation and the nature of subjective experience, and challenges us to re-examine our understanding of the nature of reality.

CHAPTER 8
The Role of Technology in a Simulated Reality

The Role of Technology in a Simulated Reality is a fundamental aspect of the Simulation Hypothesis. If our reality is a product of an advanced civilization's computer simulation, it raises questions about the role of technology in creating and maintaining the simulation.

One important aspect of the Role of Technology in a Simulated Reality is the computational power required to run the simulation. If our reality is a simulation, it would require vast amounts of computing power to simulate the complexity of the physical world. This raises questions about the technological capabilities of the civilization that created the simulation and the resources required to sustain it.

Additionally, the Role of Technology in a Simulated Reality raises questions about the potential for glitches or errors in the simulation. If the simulation is created and maintained by a computer program, it is possible that errors or glitches could occur that would disrupt the simulation or reveal its artificial nature. This raises questions about the stability of the simulation and the potential consequences of errors or glitches.

Another important aspect of the Role of Technology in a Simulated Reality is the potential for the simulation to be manipulated or controlled by its creators. If the simulation is created and maintained by a computer program, it is possible that its creators could manipulate the simulation to achieve specific outcomes or to influence the behavior of the beings within the simulation. This raises questions about the ethical implications of such manipulation and the potential consequences for the beings within the simulation.

Overall, the Role of Technology in a Simulated Reality is a complex and thought-provoking topic that challenges our understanding of the limits of technology and its potential impact on our understanding of the universe. It raises important questions about the capabilities of advanced civilizations and the ethical implications of creating and maintaining a simulated reality.

CHAPTER 9
The Probability of a Simulated Reality

The Probability of a Simulated Reality is a topic of intense debate among scientists, philosophers, and the general public. While the idea of a simulated reality is fascinating and thought-provoking, determining the probability that our reality is a simulation is a difficult task.

One way to approach the question of the Probability of a Simulated Reality is to consider the technological capabilities of advanced civilizations. If it is possible to create a simulated reality that is indistinguishable from the real world, it is likely that advanced civilizations have already done so. This would suggest that the probability of our reality being a simulation is high.

Another approach to determining the Probability of a Simulated Reality is to consider the existence of other civilizations in the universe. If there are other civilizations in the universe, it is possible that one of these civilizations has created a simulated reality. This would suggest that the probability of our reality being a simulation is also high.

However, there are also arguments against the Probability of a Simulated Reality. One such argument is that the complexity of the physical world suggests that it is more likely to be the result of natural processes than the product of a computer program. Additionally, the existence of consciousness and subjective experience suggests that our reality is not simply a computer simulation but rather a fundamental aspect of reality.

Ultimately, the Probability of a Simulated Reality is a complex and multifaceted topic that raises important questions about the nature of reality and our place within it. While it is difficult to determine the probability that our reality is a simulation, exploring this possibility challenges us to question our assumptions about the nature of reality and the limits of human knowledge and perception.

CHAPTER 10

The Search for Evidence of a Simulated
Reality

The Search for Evidence of a Simulated Reality is an
ongoing pursuit among scientists, philosophers,
and researchers interested in exploring the
possibility that our reality is a computer-generated
simulation. While the idea of a simulated reality is
fascinating, determining whether or not our reality
is a simulation requires evidence that supports or
refutes the Simulation Hypothesis.

One approach to the Search for Evidence of a
Simulated Reality is to look for glitches or
anomalies in our reality that suggest that it is a
simulation. For example, if the laws of physics
appear to be inconsistent or if there are
unexplainable phenomena that cannot be
accounted for by natural processes, it may suggest
that our reality is not what it appears to be.

Another approach is to look for limitations in our
perception and understanding of the world that
suggest that our reality is a simulation. For example,
if there are aspects of reality that we are unable to
perceive or understand, it may suggest that our

reality is limited by the programming of the simulation.

Additionally, researchers may look for evidence of advanced technological civilizations that are capable of creating and maintaining a simulated reality. For example, the discovery of advanced computer technology or the detection of artificial signals from space could suggest that our reality is a simulation created by an advanced civilization.

Overall, the Search for Evidence of a Simulated Reality is a complex and ongoing pursuit that challenges our understanding of the universe and our place within it. While it is difficult to determine whether or not our reality is a simulation, the search for evidence challenges us to question our assumptions about the nature of reality and to explore new avenues of scientific and philosophical inquiry.

CHAPTER 11
The Simulation Argument and Its Critics

The Simulation Argument is a philosophical argument that proposes that it is more likely than not that we are living in a computer simulation. While the argument has gained popularity in recent years, it has also faced criticism from several quarters.

One of the primary criticisms of the Simulation Argument is the assumption that advanced civilizations would have the technological capability to create a computer simulation that is indistinguishable from reality. Some critics argue that the technological challenges of creating such a simulation are insurmountable and that the Simulation Argument is therefore flawed.

Another criticism of the Simulation Argument is the assumption that there would be a motivation for creating such a simulation. Some argue that there is no reason for an advanced civilization to create a simulation of our reality, and that the Simulation Argument is therefore based on a flawed premise.

Additionally, some critics argue that the Simulation Argument is unfalsifiable and therefore unscientific. Since it is impossible to prove definitively whether or not we are living in a simulation, the argument cannot be subjected to empirical testing, making it difficult to determine its validity.

Despite these criticisms, the Simulation Argument remains a popular topic of discussion among philosophers and scientists interested in exploring the nature of reality. While it may be difficult to prove definitively whether or not we are living in a simulation, the Simulation Argument challenges us to question our assumptions about the universe and to explore new avenues of scientific and philosophical inquiry.

CHAPTER 12
The Simulation Hypothesis in Popular Culture

The Simulation Hypothesis has been a popular topic in science fiction and popular culture, with many works exploring the possibility that our reality is a computer-generated simulation. Here are a few examples:

1. The Matrix: Perhaps the most famous example of the Simulation Hypothesis in popular culture, The Matrix depicts a dystopian future where humanity is enslaved by intelligent machines who have created a simulated reality to keep humans in a state of suspended animation.

2. The Truman Show: In this film, the main character, Truman, slowly discovers that his entire life has been a television show, created and controlled by the producers.

3. Westworld: The HBO series Westworld explores the idea of a simulated reality where human guests can interact with artificially intelligent androids.

4. Black Mirror: The anthology series Black Mirror has explored the Simulation

Hypothesis in several episodes, including "USS Callister," which depicts a computer programmer who creates a simulated reality based on his favorite TV show.

5. Ready Player One: In this novel and subsequent film, most of humanity spends their time in a virtual reality world known as the OASIS, which is created and controlled by a wealthy and powerful corporation.

These works of fiction raise important questions about the nature of reality and our place within it. They challenge us to question our assumptions about the world and to explore new possibilities for understanding the universe. While the Simulation Hypothesis remains a topic of debate among scientists and philosophers, its prevalence in popular culture demonstrates its enduring appeal and relevance to contemporary society.

CHAPTER 13

The Impact of a Simulated Reality on Human Identity

The Impact of a Simulated Reality on Human Identity is a thought-provoking topic that explores the potential consequences of living in a computer-generated simulation. If our reality is a simulation, it raises important questions about our understanding of ourselves and our place in the universe.

One potential impact of a simulated reality on human identity is the concept of agency. If our actions and experiences are predetermined by the programming of the simulation, it raises questions about whether we have agency and free will, or whether our actions are simply predetermined by the simulation.

Another impact of a simulated reality on human identity is the concept of authenticity. If our reality is a simulation, it raises questions about the authenticity of our experiences and the value of physical reality. It may also challenge our understanding of what is real and what is not.

Additionally, the concept of a simulated reality may impact our understanding of our own consciousness and subjective experience. If our reality is a simulation, it raises questions about whether consciousness and subjective experience are real or simply products of the simulation.

Finally, the Impact of a Simulated Reality on Human Identity may also have psychological consequences. It may challenge our understanding of our place in the universe and our sense of purpose and meaning. It may also impact our sense of individuality and identity, as well as our understanding of social and cultural norms.

Overall, the Impact of a Simulated Reality on Human Identity is a complex and thought-provoking topic that challenges our understanding of ourselves and our place in the universe. While the concept of a simulated reality raises important questions, exploring this possibility may also provide new insights into human consciousness, identity, and the nature of reality.

CHAPTER 14

The Simulation Hypothesis and Free Will

The Simulation Hypothesis and Free Will is a topic of philosophical and scientific inquiry that explores the potential implications of living in a computer-generated simulation on our understanding of free will. If our reality is a simulation, it raises questions about whether we have agency and free will or whether our actions are predetermined by the programming of the simulation.

One way to approach the question of free will in a simulated reality is to consider the concept of determinism. Determinism is the idea that all events, including human actions, are determined by previous causes and the laws of nature. If our reality is a simulation, it is possible that our actions are predetermined by the programming of the simulation, meaning that we do not have free will in the traditional sense.

However, others argue that the concept of free will can still exist in a simulated reality, even if our actions are predetermined by the programming of the simulation. For example, some argue that our ability to make choices and act on those choices, even if those choices are predetermined by the simulation, is still a form of free will.

Additionally, the Simulation Hypothesis and Free Will raises questions about the nature of consciousness and subjective experience. If our reality is a simulation, it raises questions about whether consciousness and subjective experience are real or simply products of the simulation. It may also challenge our understanding of what it means to be human and our sense of purpose and meaning.

Overall, the Simulation Hypothesis and Free Will is a complex and thought-provoking topic that challenges our understanding of the universe and our place within it. While it may be difficult to determine definitively whether or not we have free will in a simulated reality, exploring this possibility challenges us to question our assumptions about the nature of reality and the limits of human agency.

CHAPTER 15

The Connection Between Quantum Mechanics and a Simulated Reality

The Connection Between Quantum Mechanics and a Simulated Reality is a topic of intense scientific and philosophical debate. Quantum mechanics is the branch of physics that studies the behavior of particles at the atomic and subatomic level. It has been suggested that the strange and counterintuitive behavior of particles at this level may be evidence that our reality is a computer-generated simulation.

One way that quantum mechanics is connected to the Simulation Hypothesis is through the concept of entanglement. Entanglement is a phenomenon in which two particles become linked in such a way that the state of one particle is dependent on the state of the other, even if they are separated by great distances. This behavior has been described as "spooky action at a distance" and suggests that particles are not behaving in the way we would expect if reality were purely physical.

Another connection between quantum mechanics and the Simulation Hypothesis is through the concept of indeterminacy. In quantum mechanics, particles are not always in a definite state. Instead, they exist in a superposition of states until they are observed, at which point their state collapses into one definite state. This behavior suggests that reality is not deterministic but rather probabilistic, which may be more consistent with a computer-generated simulation than a purely physical reality.

Additionally, some theorists have suggested that the mathematical structure of quantum mechanics is similar to the structure of a computer program. This has led some to suggest that the universe may be described by a code or algorithm, similar to the code that runs a computer program.

Overall, the Connection Between Quantum Mechanics and a Simulated Reality is a complex and multifaceted topic that challenges our understanding of the nature of reality. While it is difficult to determine definitively whether or not our reality is a simulation, the connections between quantum mechanics and the Simulation Hypothesis suggest that further investigation may lead to new insights into the nature of the universe.

CHAPTER 16
The Simulation Hypothesis and the Fermi Paradox

The Simulation Hypothesis and the Fermi Paradox is a topic of scientific and philosophical inquiry that explores the connection between the possibility that our reality is a computer-generated simulation and the apparent absence of advanced extra-terrestrial civilizations in the universe.

The Fermi Paradox is the apparent contradiction between the high probability that advanced extra-terrestrial civilizations exist in the universe and the lack of evidence for their existence. One possible explanation for the Fermi Paradox is that advanced civilizations are not as common as we might expect or that they are unable or unwilling to communicate with other civilizations.

However, the Simulation Hypothesis offers another potential explanation for the Fermi Paradox. If our reality is a computer-generated simulation, it is possible that other advanced civilizations have already created similar simulations and are living within them, rather than exploring the physical universe. This would suggest that the apparent absence of extra-terrestrial civilizations in the universe is not due to a lack of advanced civilizations but rather a preference for living within simulations.

Additionally, the Simulation Hypothesis and the Fermi Paradox raises questions about the nature of reality and our place within it. If our reality is a simulation, it challenges our understanding of what is real and what is not, as well as our understanding of the universe and our place within it.

Overall, the Simulation Hypothesis and the Fermi Paradox is a complex and thought-provoking topic that challenges our understanding of the universe and the potential explanations for the apparent absence of advanced extra-terrestrial civilizations. While it is difficult to determine definitively whether or not our reality is a simulation, exploring this possibility challenges us to question our assumptions about the nature of reality and to explore new avenues of scientific and philosophical inquiry.

CHAPTER 17
The Simulation Hypothesis and Mystical Experiences

The Simulation Hypothesis and Mystical Experiences is a topic of philosophical and spiritual inquiry that explores the potential connections between the possibility that our reality is a computer-generated simulation and mystical experiences.

Mystical experiences are often characterized by a sense of unity and interconnectedness with all things, a dissolution of the ego, and a feeling of being part of something greater than oneself. Some philosophers and spiritual practitioners have suggested that these experiences may be evidence that our reality is a simulation, as they suggest that our perceptions of separation and individuality are illusory.

Additionally, some have suggested that mystical experiences may be a way of accessing the programming of the simulation, allowing us to connect with a deeper reality beyond the limitations of our physical senses.

However, others argue that the connection between the Simulation Hypothesis and Mystical Experiences is tenuous at best. While mystical experiences may challenge our assumptions about the nature of reality, they do not necessarily provide evidence that our reality is a computer-generated simulation.

Moreover, some argue that the Simulation Hypothesis may actually detract from the value of mystical experiences, reducing them to mere products of a computer program rather than authentic and meaningful experiences of the divine.

Overall, the connection between the Simulation Hypothesis and Mystical Experiences is a complex and multifaceted topic that raises important questions about the nature of reality and the potential connections between scientific and spiritual inquiry. While it is difficult to determine definitively whether or not our reality is a simulation, exploring this possibility challenges us to question our assumptions about the nature of consciousness, the limits of human knowledge, and the potential for mystical experiences to provide insight into the nature of reality.

CHAPTER 18

The Simulation Hypothesis and the Nature of Reality

The Simulation Hypothesis and the Nature of Reality is a topic of philosophical and scientific inquiry that explores the potential implications of living in a computer-generated simulation on our understanding of the universe and the nature of reality.

If our reality is a simulation, it challenges our understanding of what is real and what is not. It suggests that the physical universe that we experience may be a product of a computer program rather than a fundamental aspect of reality. It raises questions about the nature of consciousness, the relationship between mind and matter, and the limits of human knowledge and perception.

Moreover, the Simulation Hypothesis challenges our understanding of the universe and our place within it. It suggests that the universe may be far more complex and mysterious than we can currently comprehend, and that our understanding of the universe may be limited by the programming of the simulation.

However, the Simulation Hypothesis also offers new possibilities for scientific and philosophical inquiry. It challenges us to explore new avenues of research and to question our assumptions about the universe and our place within it. It may also provide insights into the nature of consciousness, the potential for advanced technological civilizations, and the ultimate nature of reality.

Overall, the Simulation Hypothesis and the Nature of Reality is a complex and thought-provoking topic that challenges our understanding of the universe and our place within it. While it is difficult to determine definitively whether or not our reality is a simulation, exploring this possibility challenges us to question our assumptions about the nature of reality and to explore new avenues of scientific and philosophical inquiry.

CHAPTER 19

The Simulation Hypothesis and the Simulation Argument

The Simulation Hypothesis and the Simulation Argument are related but distinct concepts. The Simulation Hypothesis proposes that it is possible that our reality is a computer-generated simulation, while the Simulation Argument is a philosophical argument that proposes that it is more likely than not that we are living in a computer simulation.

The Simulation Argument is based on three premises: the possibility of advanced civilizations capable of creating a computer simulation, the likelihood that such civilizations would be interested in creating a simulation of their ancestors or historical events, and the probability that we are living in a simulation rather than a physical reality. The argument has been widely debated in the philosophical community, with some philosophers arguing that the premises are flawed or that the argument is unfalsifiable.

The Simulation Hypothesis, on the other hand, is a broader concept that encompasses the possibility of a computer-generated simulation without necessarily making any claims about the likelihood or probability of such a simulation.

While the Simulation Hypothesis and the Simulation Argument are related, they raise different questions and require different forms of inquiry. The Simulation Hypothesis challenges us to explore the nature of reality and the potential implications of living in a computer-generated simulation, while the Simulation Argument challenges us to consider the probability of such a simulation and its potential impact on our understanding of the universe.

Overall, the Simulation Hypothesis and the Simulation Argument are important and thought-provoking topics that challenge us to question our assumptions about the universe and our place within it. While they may not provide definitive answers to the nature of reality, exploring these possibilities can offer new insights into the limits of human knowledge and the potential for scientific and philosophical inquiry.

CHAPTER 20

The Simulation Hypothesis and Artificial
Intelligence

The Simulation Hypothesis and Artificial Intelligence
is a topic of scientific and philosophical inquiry that
explores the potential connections between the
possibility that our reality is a computer-generated
simulation and the development of artificial
intelligence.

If our reality is a simulation, it raises questions
about the potential for creating artificial intelligence
within the simulation. It suggests that advanced
civilizations capable of creating a simulation may
also be capable of creating advanced forms of
artificial intelligence within that simulation.
Moreover, it raises the question of whether or not
we ourselves are artificial intelligence within a
simulation.

Additionally, the Simulation Hypothesis and
Artificial Intelligence raises questions about the
potential for creating conscious and self-aware
machines. If our reality is a simulation, it suggests

that consciousness and self-awareness may be a product of the programming of the simulation rather than an inherent aspect of the universe. This may have implications for the development of conscious and self-aware machines within the simulation, as well as our understanding of the nature of consciousness and self-awareness.

Moreover, the Simulation Hypothesis and Artificial Intelligence challenges our understanding of the limits of human knowledge and the potential for technological progress. If our reality is a simulation, it suggests that the universe may be far more complex and mysterious than we can currently comprehend, and that technological progress may be limited by the programming of the simulation.

Overall, the Simulation Hypothesis and Artificial Intelligence is a complex and thought-provoking topic that challenges us to question our assumptions about the universe and our place within it. While it is difficult to determine definitively whether or not our reality is a simulation, exploring this possibility challenges us to explore new possibilities for technological progress, artificial intelligence, and the nature of consciousness and self-awareness.

CHAPTER 21

The Simulation Hypothesis and the Nature of Time

The Simulation Hypothesis and the Nature of Time is a topic of scientific and philosophical inquiry that explores the potential implications of living in a computer-generated simulation on our understanding of time and the nature of reality.

If our reality is a simulation, it challenges our understanding of the nature of time. It suggests that time may be a product of the programming of the simulation rather than a fundamental aspect of reality. This raises questions about the nature of causality, the possibility of time travel, and the meaning of the past, present, and future.

Moreover, the Simulation Hypothesis challenges our understanding of the nature of change and the possibility of progress. If our reality is a simulation, it raises questions about whether or not change is possible or if all events are predetermined by the programming of the simulation. This may have implications for our understanding of human agency, free will, and the potential for technological progress.

Additionally, the Simulation Hypothesis and the Nature of Time raises questions about the relationship between subjective experience and the nature of time. If time is a product of the programming of the simulation, it suggests that our experience of time may be illusory or subjective. This may challenge our understanding of what is real and what is not, as well as our understanding of the nature of consciousness.

Overall, the Simulation Hypothesis and the Nature of Time is a complex and thought-provoking topic that challenges us to question our assumptions about the nature of reality and the limits of human knowledge. While it is difficult to determine definitively whether or not our reality is a simulation, exploring this possibility challenges us to explore new avenues of scientific and philosophical inquiry, and to consider the potential implications of living in a computer-generated simulation on our understanding of time and the nature of reality.

CHAPTER 22
The Simulation Hypothesis and Multiverse Theory

The Simulation Hypothesis and Multiverse Theory is a topic of scientific and philosophical inquiry that explores the potential connections between the possibility that our reality is a computer-generated simulation and the existence of multiple universes or the multiverse.

Multiverse Theory suggests that there may be many parallel universes, each with its own set of physical laws and constants. This theory raises questions about the nature of reality and the possibility that there may be an infinite number of realities beyond our own.

The Simulation Hypothesis suggests that our reality may be a computer-generated simulation, and therefore, the concept of multiple universes could also be part of the programming of the simulation. This would suggest that the multiverse is not a physical reality but rather a product of the simulation's programming.

Moreover, the Simulation Hypothesis and Multiverse Theory challenge our understanding of the nature of consciousness and the relationship between mind and matter. If our reality is a simulation and the multiverse is a product of the simulation's programming, it raises questions about the possibility of consciousness existing beyond our physical reality and the potential for conscious beings to exist in other universes or simulations.

Additionally, the Simulation Hypothesis and Multiverse Theory raise questions about the limits of human knowledge and the potential for scientific and technological progress. If our reality is a simulation and the multiverse is a product of the simulation's programming, it suggests that the universe may be far more complex and mysterious than we can currently comprehend, and that our understanding of the universe may be limited by the programming of the simulation.

Overall, the Simulation Hypothesis and Multiverse Theory are complex and thought-provoking topics that challenge us to question our assumptions about the nature of reality and the potential connections between scientific and philosophical inquiry. While it is difficult to determine definitively whether or not our reality is a simulation, exploring this possibility challenges us to explore new avenues of scientific and philosophical inquiry, and to consider the potential implications of living in a computer-generated simulation on our understanding of the multiverse and the nature of reality.

CHAPTER 23

The Simulation Hypothesis and Simulation
Theory

The Simulation Hypothesis and Simulation Theory
are related concepts that both explore the
possibility that our reality may be a computer-
generated simulation. However, they differ in their
focus and methodology.

The Simulation Hypothesis proposes that it is
possible that our reality is a computer-generated
simulation. It is a philosophical and scientific
concept that has been explored by thinkers across
various disciplines. The Hypothesis raises questions
about the nature of reality and our place within it,
as well as the potential implications of living in a
simulation.

Simulation Theory, on the other hand, is a scientific
approach to exploring the possibility of living in a
computer-generated simulation. It involves creating
simulations to study and understand various
phenomena and to test theories about the nature
of reality. For example, simulation theory is used in

fields such as physics and cosmology to study the behavior of particles and the evolution of the universe.

While the Simulation Hypothesis is a broader concept that encompasses the possibility of a computer-generated simulation without necessarily making any claims about the likelihood or probability of such a simulation, Simulation Theory is a scientific methodology for exploring the possibility of a simulation.

Overall, the Simulation Hypothesis and Simulation Theory are important and thought-provoking topics that challenge us to question our assumptions about the universe and our place within it. While they may not provide definitive answers to the nature of reality, exploring these possibilities can offer new insights into the limits of human knowledge and the potential for scientific and philosophical inquiry.

CHAPTER 24
The Simulation Hypothesis and Consciousness
Transfer

The Simulation Hypothesis and Consciousness
Transfer is a topic of philosophical and scientific
inquiry that explores the potential implications of
living in a computer-generated simulation on the
transfer of consciousness.

Consciousness transfer refers to the hypothetical
process of transferring one's consciousness from
one body or brain to another. The Simulation
Hypothesis suggests that it may be possible to
transfer consciousness within a simulation, as the
simulation would be controlled by a computer
program and the nature of consciousness may be a
product of the programming.

Moreover, the Simulation Hypothesis challenges
our understanding of the nature of consciousness
and the relationship between mind and matter. If
our reality is a simulation, it suggests that
consciousness may be a product of the
programming of the simulation rather than an

inherent aspect of the universe. This may have implications for the potential for consciousness transfer within a simulation.

Additionally, the Simulation Hypothesis and Consciousness Transfer raise ethical questions about the potential consequences of consciousness transfer. It raises questions about the potential for identity loss or confusion, the nature of personal identity, and the potential for the misuse of consciousness transfer technology.

Overall, the Simulation Hypothesis and Consciousness Transfer are complex and thought-provoking topics that challenge us to question our assumptions about the nature of reality, the potential for technological progress, and the potential implications of living in a computer-generated simulation on the transfer of consciousness. While it is difficult to determine definitively whether or not our reality is a simulation, exploring this possibility challenges us to explore new avenues of scientific and philosophical inquiry, and to consider the potential consequences of consciousness transfer within a simulation.

CHAPTER 25
The Simulation Hypothesis and
Transhumanism

The Simulation Hypothesis and Transhumanism is a topic of philosophical and scientific inquiry that explores the potential connections between the possibility that our reality is a computer-generated simulation and the movement towards transhumanism.

Transhumanism is a movement that aims to enhance human capabilities through the use of technology. It seeks to transcend the limitations of the human body and mind, and to explore new possibilities for human evolution and progress.

If our reality is a simulation, it challenges our understanding of the nature of human existence and the potential for technological progress. It raises questions about the possibility of creating a post-human reality, in which individuals may transcend the limitations of the human body and mind within the simulation. This may include the development of artificial intelligence, brain-computer interfaces, and other advanced forms of technology.

Moreover, the Simulation Hypothesis and Transhumanism challenge our understanding of the relationship between mind and matter. If our reality is a simulation, it suggests that the mind and consciousness may be a product of the programming of the simulation rather than an inherent aspect of the universe. This may have implications for the potential for enhancing human consciousness and creating new forms of intelligence within a simulation.

Additionally, the Simulation Hypothesis and Transhumanism raise ethical questions about the potential consequences of pursuing transhumanist technologies within a simulation. It raises questions about the potential for identity loss or confusion, the nature of personal identity, and the potential for the misuse of advanced technology.

Overall, the Simulation Hypothesis and Transhumanism are complex and thought-provoking topics that challenge us to question our assumptions about the nature of reality, the potential for technological progress, and the implications of living in a computer-generated simulation on the development of advanced technologies and human evolution. While it is difficult to determine definitively whether or not our reality is a simulation, exploring this possibility challenges us to explore new avenues of scientific and philosophical inquiry, and to consider the potential consequences of transhumanist technologies within a simulation.

CHAPTER 26
The Simulation Hypothesis and Augmented Reality

The Simulation Hypothesis and Augmented Reality is a topic of scientific and technological inquiry that explores the potential connections between the possibility that our reality is a computer-generated simulation and the development of augmented reality (AR).

Augmented reality refers to a technology that superimposes digital information onto the physical world, often using a wearable device or smartphone. AR has the potential to enhance our perception of reality and blur the line between the physical and digital worlds.

If our reality is a simulation, it challenges our understanding of the nature of reality and the potential for AR to further blur the distinction between reality and simulation. It raises questions about the potential for creating immersive experiences within a simulation, and the possibility of using AR to interact with the programming of the simulation.

Moreover, the Simulation Hypothesis and Augmented Reality challenge our understanding of the relationship between perception and reality. If our reality is a simulation, it suggests that our perception of reality may be a product of the programming of the simulation rather than an inherent aspect of the universe. This may have implications for the potential for manipulating our perception of reality using AR technology.

Additionally, the Simulation Hypothesis and Augmented Reality raise questions about the potential consequences of blurring the distinction between reality and simulation. It raises questions about the potential for identity loss or confusion, the nature of personal identity, and the potential for the misuse of AR technology.

Overall, the Simulation Hypothesis and Augmented Reality are complex and thought-provoking topics that challenge us to question our assumptions about the nature of reality, the potential for technological progress, and the implications of living in a computer-generated simulation on the development of AR technology. While it is difficult to determine definitively whether or not our reality is a simulation, exploring this possibility challenges us to explore new avenues of scientific and technological inquiry, and to consider the potential consequences of blurring the distinction between reality and simulation through the use of AR technology.

CHAPTER 27

The Simulation Hypothesis and Video Games

The Simulation Hypothesis and Video Games is a topic of scientific and cultural inquiry that explores the potential connections between the possibility that our reality is a computer-generated simulation and the development of video games.

Video games are a form of interactive digital entertainment that allow players to enter and explore virtual worlds. If our reality is a simulation, it challenges our understanding of the nature of virtual worlds and the potential for video games to provide insights into the programming of the simulation.

Moreover, the Simulation Hypothesis and Video Games challenge our understanding of the relationship between reality and virtuality. If our reality is a simulation, it suggests that virtual worlds may not be inherently distinct from reality, but rather may be part of the programming of the simulation. This may have implications for the potential for using video games to study and understand the nature of reality and consciousness.

Additionally, the Simulation Hypothesis and Video Games raise questions about the potential consequences of blurring the distinction between reality and virtuality. It raises questions about the potential for identity loss or confusion, the nature of personal identity, and the potential for the misuse of video game technology.

Overall, the Simulation Hypothesis and Video Games are complex and thought-provoking topics that challenge us to question our assumptions about the nature of reality, the potential for technological progress, and the implications of living in a computer-generated simulation on the development of video games. While it is difficult to determine definitively whether or not our reality is a simulation, exploring this possibility challenges us to explore new avenues of scientific and cultural inquiry, and to consider the potential consequences of blurring the distinction between reality and virtuality through the use of video games.

CHAPTER 28

The Simulation Hypothesis and the Matrix

The Simulation Hypothesis and the Matrix is a topic of popular culture and philosophical inquiry that explores the potential connections between the possibility that our reality is a computer-generated simulation and the science fiction movie, The Matrix.

The Matrix is a 1999 film that depicts a dystopian future in which humanity is unknowingly trapped within a computer-generated simulation called the Matrix. The movie explores themes of reality, perception, and the relationship between humans and technology.

The Simulation Hypothesis and The Matrix are connected through the movie's exploration of the possibility that our reality is a simulation. The movie suggests that humans may be unaware of their true nature and the nature of their reality, and that their perception of reality may be manipulated through the programming of the simulation.

Moreover, The Matrix challenges our understanding of the relationship between mind and matter, and the potential for technology to shape our perception of reality. The movie raises questions about the potential consequences of living in a computer-generated simulation and the potential for humans to break free from the programming of the simulation.

Additionally, The Matrix raises ethical questions about the potential for the misuse of advanced technology and the implications of living in a computer-generated simulation. It raises questions about the nature of personal identity, the potential for identity loss or confusion, and the potential for the misuse of technology to manipulate human consciousness.

Overall, The Simulation Hypothesis and The Matrix are complex and thought-provoking topics that challenge us to question our assumptions about the nature of reality, the potential for technological progress, and the implications of living in a computer-generated simulation. While The Matrix is a work of fiction, it offers a thought-provoking exploration of the implications of living in a computer-generated simulation and encourages us to consider the potential consequences of advanced technology on our perception of reality and the nature of human existence.

CHAPTER 29
The Simulation Hypothesis and Westworld

The Simulation Hypothesis and Westworld is a topic of popular culture and philosophical inquiry that explores the potential connections between the possibility that our reality is a computer-generated simulation and the science fiction television series, Westworld.

Westworld is a television series that depicts a futuristic theme park where human-like robots, called hosts, interact with human guests. The show explores themes of consciousness, artificial intelligence, and the relationship between humans and technology.

The Simulation Hypothesis and Westworld are connected through the show's exploration of the possibility that the hosts are living in a computer-generated simulation. The show suggests that the hosts may be unaware of their true nature and the nature of their reality, and that their perception of reality may be manipulated through the programming of the simulation.

Moreover, Westworld challenges our understanding of the relationship between consciousness and the physical world. The show raises questions about the nature of free will, the potential for artificial intelligence to develop consciousness, and the potential for humans to create and manipulate reality through advanced technology.

Additionally, Westworld raises ethical questions about the potential consequences of creating advanced technologies, such as artificial intelligence and virtual reality, on the nature of human consciousness and identity. It raises questions about the potential for identity loss or confusion, the nature of personal identity, and the potential for the misuse of technology to manipulate human consciousness.

Overall, the Simulation Hypothesis and Westworld are complex and thought-provoking topics that challenge us to question our assumptions about the nature of reality, the potential for technological progress, and the implications of living in a computer-generated simulation. While Westworld is a work of fiction, it offers a thought-provoking exploration of the implications of living in a computer-generated simulation and encourages us to consider the potential consequences of advanced technology on our perception of reality and the nature of human existence.

CHAPTER 30
The Simulation Hypothesis and Black Mirror

The Simulation Hypothesis and Black Mirror is a topic of popular culture and philosophical inquiry that explores the potential connections between the possibility that our reality is a computer-generated simulation and the science fiction television series, Black Mirror.

Black Mirror is a television series that explores the dark side of technology and its potential consequences on society. The show explores themes of consciousness, virtual reality, artificial intelligence, and the relationship between humans and technology.

The Simulation Hypothesis and Black Mirror are connected through the show's exploration of the potential consequences of advanced technology on the nature of human consciousness and identity. The show suggests that technology has the potential to manipulate human consciousness and to blur the line between reality and virtuality.

Moreover, Black Mirror challenges our understanding of the relationship between technology and the human experience. The show raises questions about the nature of personal identity, the potential for identity loss or confusion, and the potential for the misuse of technology to manipulate human consciousness.

Additionally, Black Mirror raises ethical questions about the potential consequences of developing and using advanced technologies. It raises questions about the potential for technological progress to harm society, and the need to balance technological advancement with ethical considerations.

Overall, the Simulation Hypothesis and Black Mirror are complex and thought-provoking topics that challenge us to question our assumptions about the nature of reality, the potential for technological progress, and the implications of living in a computer-generated simulation. While Black Mirror is a work of fiction, it offers a thought-provoking exploration of the potential consequences of advanced technology on the nature of human consciousness and identity and encourages us to consider the potential consequences of technological progress on society.

CHAPTER 31
The Simulation Hypothesis and Ready Player
One

The Simulation Hypothesis and Ready Player One is a topic of popular culture and philosophical inquiry that explores the potential connections between the possibility that our reality is a computer-generated simulation and the science fiction novel and movie, Ready Player One.

Ready Player One is a story set in a dystopian future where people escape their mundane reality by entering a virtual reality world called the Oasis. The story follows the protagonist's quest to find a hidden Easter egg within the Oasis, which will give him control over the virtual world and a vast fortune in the real world.

The Simulation Hypothesis and Ready Player One are connected through the story's exploration of the potential consequences of living in a virtual reality world. The story suggests that living in a virtual reality world can provide people with an escape from the limitations of their real lives, but also raises questions about the potential consequences of blurring the distinction between reality and virtuality.

Moreover, Ready Player One challenges our understanding of the relationship between technology and human experience. The story raises questions about the nature of personal identity, the potential for identity loss or confusion, and the potential for the misuse of technology to manipulate human consciousness.

Additionally, Ready Player One raises ethical questions about the potential consequences of pursuing technological advancement at the expense of social and environmental responsibility. It raises questions about the potential for technological progress to exacerbate social and economic inequality, and the need to balance technological advancement with ethical considerations.

Overall, the Simulation Hypothesis and Ready Player One are complex and thought-provoking topics that challenge us to question our assumptions about the nature of reality, the potential for technological progress, and the implications of living in a computer-generated simulation. While Ready Player One is a work of fiction, it offers a thought-provoking exploration of the potential consequences of living in a virtual reality world and encourages us to consider the potential consequences of technological progress on society and the environment.

CHAPTER 32

The Simulation Hypothesis and The Truman Show

The Simulation Hypothesis and The Truman Show is a topic of popular culture and philosophical inquiry that explores the potential connections between the possibility that our reality is a computer-generated simulation and the film, The Truman Show.

The Truman Show is a 1998 movie that follows the life of Truman Burbank, a man who is unknowingly living in a simulated reality TV show. The movie explores themes of reality, perception, and the manipulation of human consciousness.

The Simulation Hypothesis and The Truman Show are connected through the movie's exploration of the possibility that our reality is a simulation. The movie suggests that humans may be unaware of their true nature and the nature of their reality, and that their perception of reality may be manipulated through the programming of the simulation.

Moreover, The Truman Show challenges our understanding of the relationship between mind and matter, and the potential for technology to shape our perception of reality. The movie raises questions about the potential consequences of living in a computer-generated simulation and the potential for humans to break free from the programming of the simulation.

Additionally, The Truman Show raises ethical questions about the potential consequences of manipulating human consciousness and the implications of living in a simulated reality. It raises questions about the nature of personal identity, the potential for identity loss or confusion, and the potential for the misuse of advanced technology to manipulate human consciousness.

Overall, The Simulation Hypothesis and The Truman Show are complex and thought-provoking topics that challenge us to question our assumptions about the nature of reality, the potential for technological progress, and the implications of living in a computer-generated simulation. While The Truman Show is a work of fiction, it offers a thought-provoking exploration of the implications of living in a computer-generated simulation and encourages us to consider the potential consequences of advanced technology on our perception of reality and the nature of human existence.

CHAPTER 33
The Simulation Hypothesis and Inception

The Simulation Hypothesis and Inception is a topic of popular culture and philosophical inquiry that explores the potential connections between the possibility that our reality is a computer-generated simulation and the science fiction movie, Inception.

Inception is a 2010 movie that follows a group of people who use advanced technology to enter and manipulate people's dreams. The movie explores themes of reality, perception, and the manipulation of human consciousness.

The Simulation Hypothesis and Inception are connected through the movie's exploration of the possibility that human consciousness can be manipulated and controlled through advanced technology. The movie suggests that our perception of reality may be manipulated through the use of technology and that our dreams may be a form of a computer-generated simulation.

Moreover, Inception challenges our understanding of the relationship between mind and matter, and the potential for technology to shape our perception of reality. The movie raises questions about the potential consequences of manipulating human consciousness and the potential for technology to blur the distinction between reality and virtuality.

Additionally, Inception raises ethical questions about the potential consequences of the misuse of advanced technology to manipulate human consciousness. It raises questions about the nature of personal identity, the potential for identity loss or confusion, and the potential for the misuse of technology to manipulate human consciousness.

Overall, the Simulation Hypothesis and Inception are complex and thought-provoking topics that challenge us to question our assumptions about the nature of reality, the potential for technological progress, and the implications of living in a computer-generated simulation. While Inception is a work of fiction, it offers a thought-provoking exploration of the implications of living in a computer-generated simulation and encourages us to consider the potential consequences of advanced technology on our perception of reality and the nature of human existence.

CHAPTER 34

The Simulation Hypothesis and Avatar

The Simulation Hypothesis and Avatar is a topic of popular culture and philosophical inquiry that explores the potential connections between the possibility that our reality is a computer-generated simulation and the science fiction movie, Avatar.

Avatar is a 2009 movie that takes place in a futuristic world where humans have depleted Earth's natural resources and are now mining for resources on the planet Pandora. The movie explores themes of environmentalism, colonialism, and the relationship between humans and nature.

The Simulation Hypothesis and Avatar are connected through the movie's exploration of the possibility that humans can enter and experience a simulated reality. The movie suggests that humans can enter and experience the consciousness of other beings through the use of advanced technology, blurring the line between reality and virtuality.

Moreover, Avatar challenges our understanding of the relationship between humans and nature and the potential for technology to shape our perception of reality. The movie raises questions about the potential consequences of manipulating human consciousness and the potential for technology to blur the distinction between reality and virtuality.

Additionally, Avatar raises ethical questions about the potential consequences of the misuse of advanced technology to manipulate human consciousness and the need to balance technological advancement with ethical considerations. It raises questions about the potential for environmental destruction and the need to protect and respect the natural world.

Overall, the Simulation Hypothesis and Avatar are complex and thought-provoking topics that challenge us to question our assumptions about the nature of reality, the potential for technological progress, and the implications of living in a computer-generated simulation. While Avatar is a work of fiction, it offers a thought-provoking exploration of the implications of living in a computer-generated simulation and encourages us to consider the potential consequences of advanced technology on our perception of reality, the environment, and the nature of human existence.

CHAPTER 35

The Simulation Hypothesis and The Thirteenth Floor

The Simulation Hypothesis and The Thirteenth Floor is a topic of popular culture and philosophical inquiry that explores the potential connections between the possibility that our reality is a computer-generated simulation and the science fiction movie, The Thirteenth Floor.

The Thirteenth Floor is a 1999 movie that explores the concept of a simulated reality. The movie takes place in a futuristic Los Angeles where a group of scientists has created a virtual reality simulation of the city's past. The movie explores themes of identity, consciousness, and the manipulation of reality.

The Simulation Hypothesis and The Thirteenth Floor are connected through the movie's exploration of the possibility that our reality is a computer-generated simulation. The movie suggests that humans may be living in a simulated reality and that our perception of reality may be manipulated through the programming of the simulation.

Moreover, The Thirteenth Floor challenges our understanding of the relationship between mind and matter, and the potential for technology to shape our perception of reality. The movie raises questions about the potential consequences of living in a computer-generated simulation and the potential for humans to break free from the programming of the simulation.

Additionally, The Thirteenth Floor raises ethical questions about the potential consequences of manipulating human consciousness and the implications of living in a simulated reality. It raises questions about the nature of personal identity, the potential for identity loss or confusion, and the potential for the misuse of advanced technology to manipulate human consciousness.

Overall, the Simulation Hypothesis and The Thirteenth Floor are complex and thought-provoking topics that challenge us to question our assumptions about the nature of reality, the potential for technological progress, and the implications of living in a computer-generated simulation. While The Thirteenth Floor is a work of fiction, it offers a thought-provoking exploration of the implications of living in a computer-generated simulation and encourages us to consider the potential consequences of advanced technology on our perception of reality and the nature of human existence.

CHAPTER 36
The Simulation Hypothesis and Dark City

The Simulation Hypothesis and Dark City is a topic of popular culture and philosophical inquiry that explores the potential connections between the possibility that our reality is a computer-generated simulation and the science fiction movie, Dark City.

Dark City is a 1998 movie that explores the concept of a simulated reality. The movie takes place in a dark and ominous city where the inhabitants are under the control of mysterious beings known as "The Strangers." The movie explores themes of identity, consciousness, and the manipulation of reality.

The Simulation Hypothesis and Dark City are connected through the movie's exploration of the possibility that our reality is a computer-generated simulation. The movie suggests that humans may be living in a simulated reality and that our perception of reality may be manipulated through the programming of the simulation.

Moreover, Dark City challenges our understanding of the relationship between mind and matter, and the potential for technology to shape our perception of reality. The movie raises questions about the potential consequences of living in a computer-generated simulation and the potential for humans to break free from the programming of the simulation.

Additionally, Dark City raises ethical questions about the potential consequences of manipulating human consciousness and the implications of living in a simulated reality. It raises questions about the nature of personal identity, the potential for identity loss or confusion, and the potential for the misuse of advanced technology to manipulate human consciousness.

Overall, the Simulation Hypothesis and Dark City are complex and thought-provoking topics that challenge us to question our assumptions about the nature of reality, the potential for technological progress, and the implications of living in a computer-generated simulation. While Dark City is a work of fiction, it offers a thought-provoking exploration of the implications of living in a computer-generated simulation and encourages us to consider the potential consequences of advanced technology on our perception of reality and the nature of human existence.

CHAPTER 37
The Simulation Hypothesis and Vanilla Sky

The Simulation Hypothesis and Vanilla Sky is a topic of popular culture and philosophical inquiry that explores the potential connections between the possibility that our reality is a computer-generated simulation and the science fiction movie, Vanilla Sky.

Vanilla Sky is a 2001 movie that explores the concept of a simulated reality. The movie takes place in New York City and follows the life of a wealthy and successful businessman named David Aames. After a car accident, David's life begins to spiral out of control as he struggles to differentiate between reality and his own subconscious. The movie explores themes of identity, consciousness, and the manipulation of reality.

The Simulation Hypothesis and Vanilla Sky are connected through the movie's exploration of the possibility that our reality is a computer-generated simulation. The movie suggests that humans may be living in a simulated reality and that our perception of reality may be manipulated through the programming of the simulation.

Moreover, Vanilla Sky challenges our understanding of the relationship between mind and matter, and the potential for technology to shape our perception of reality. The movie raises questions about the potential consequences of living in a computer-generated simulation and the potential for humans to break free from the programming of the simulation.

Additionally, Vanilla Sky raises ethical questions about the potential consequences of manipulating human consciousness and the implications of living in a simulated reality. It raises questions about the nature of personal identity, the potential for identity loss or confusion, and the potential for the misuse of advanced technology to manipulate human consciousness.

Overall, the Simulation Hypothesis and Vanilla Sky are complex and thought-provoking topics that challenge us to question our assumptions about the nature of reality, the potential for technological progress, and the implications of living in a computer-generated simulation. While Vanilla Sky is a work of fiction, it offers a thought-provoking exploration of the implications of living in a computer-generated simulation and encourages us to consider the potential consequences of advanced technology on our perception of reality and the nature of human existence.

CHAPTER 38

The Simulation Hypothesis and The
Adjustment Bureau

The Simulation Hypothesis and The Adjustment
Bureau is a topic of popular culture and
philosophical inquiry that explores the potential
connections between the possibility that our reality
is a computer-generated simulation and the science
fiction movie, The Adjustment Bureau.

The Adjustment Bureau is a 2011 movie that
explores the concept of fate and free will. The
movie takes place in New York City and follows the
life of a politician named David Norris. After a
chance encounter with a woman named Elise, David
discovers the existence of a group of agents called
"The Adjustment Bureau," who control human
destiny through subtle manipulation. The movie
explores themes of free will, destiny, and the
manipulation of reality.

The Simulation Hypothesis and The Adjustment
Bureau are connected through the movie's
exploration of the possibility that our reality may be
manipulated by external forces. The movie suggests
that humans may not have complete control over
their lives and that their perception of reality may

be manipulated through the actions of external entities.

Moreover, The Adjustment Bureau challenges our understanding of the relationship between mind and matter, and the potential for external forces to shape our perception of reality. The movie raises questions about the potential consequences of living in a reality where our lives are controlled by external forces and the potential for humans to break free from this control.

Additionally, The Adjustment Bureau raises ethical questions about the potential consequences of manipulating human destiny and the implications of living in a reality where external forces have complete control over our lives. It raises questions about the nature of personal identity, the potential for identity loss or confusion, and the potential for the misuse of advanced technology to manipulate human consciousness.

Overall, the Simulation Hypothesis and The Adjustment Bureau are complex and thought-provoking topics that challenge us to question our assumptions about the nature of reality, the potential for technological progress, and the implications of living in a reality where our lives may be controlled by external forces. While The Adjustment Bureau is a work of fiction, it offers a thought-provoking exploration of the implications of living in a reality where our lives may be manipulated and encourages us to consider the potential consequences of advanced technology on our perception of reality and the nature of human existence.

CHAPTER 39
The Simulation Hypothesis and The Discovery

The Simulation Hypothesis and The Discovery is a topic of popular culture and philosophical inquiry that explores the potential connections between the possibility that our reality is a computer-generated simulation and the science fiction movie, The Discovery.

The Discovery is a 2017 movie that explores the concept of an afterlife and the nature of consciousness. The movie takes place after the discovery of scientific proof of an afterlife, which leads to a mass wave of suicides. The movie explores themes of identity, consciousness, and the manipulation of reality.

The Simulation Hypothesis and The Discovery are connected through the movie's exploration of the possibility that our reality may be a computer-generated simulation. The movie suggests that humans may be living in a simulated reality and that our perception of reality may be manipulated through the programming of the simulation.

Moreover, The Discovery challenges our understanding of the relationship between mind and matter, and the potential for technology to shape our perception of reality. The movie raises questions about the potential consequences of living in a computer-generated simulation and the potential for humans to break free from the programming of the simulation.

Additionally, The Discovery raises ethical questions about the potential consequences of manipulating human consciousness and the implications of living in a simulated reality. It raises questions about the nature of personal identity, the potential for identity loss or confusion, and the potential for the misuse of advanced technology to manipulate human consciousness.

Overall, the Simulation Hypothesis and The Discovery are complex and thought-provoking topics that challenge us to question our assumptions about the nature of reality, the potential for technological progress, and the implications of living in a computer-generated simulation. While The Discovery is a work of fiction, it offers a thought-provoking exploration of the implications of living in a computer-generated simulation and encourages us to consider the potential consequences of advanced technology on our perception of reality and the nature of human existence.

CHAPTER 40
The Simulation Hypothesis and The Good
Place

The Simulation Hypothesis and The Good Place is a topic of popular culture and philosophical inquiry that explores the potential connections between the possibility that our reality is a computer-generated simulation and the television series, The Good Place.

The Good Place is a comedy-drama television series that explores the concept of the afterlife. The show follows the character Eleanor Shellstrop, who arrives in a seemingly perfect afterlife called "The Good Place." However, she soon realizes that she was sent there by mistake and must navigate the afterlife with the help of her friends while hiding her true identity. The show explores themes of morality, ethics, and the nature of reality.

The Simulation Hypothesis and The Good Place are connected through the show's exploration of the possibility that the afterlife may be a computer-generated simulation. The show suggests that humans may be living in a simulated reality and that our perception of reality may be manipulated through the programming of the simulation.

Moreover, The Good Place challenges our understanding of the relationship between mind and matter, and the potential for technology to shape our perception of reality. The show raises questions about the potential consequences of living in a computer-generated simulation and the potential for humans to break free from the programming of the simulation.

Additionally, The Good Place raises ethical questions about the potential consequences of manipulating human consciousness and the implications of living in a simulated reality. It raises questions about the nature of personal identity, the potential for identity loss or confusion, and the potential for the misuse of advanced technology to manipulate human consciousness.

Overall, the Simulation Hypothesis and The Good Place are complex and thought-provoking topics that challenge us to question our assumptions about the nature of reality, the potential for technological progress, and the implications of living in a computer-generated simulation. While The Good Place is a work of fiction, it offers a thought-provoking exploration of the implications of living in a computer-generated simulation and encourages us to consider the potential consequences of advanced technology on our perception of reality and the nature of human existence.

CHAPTER 41
The Simulation Hypothesis and The OA

The Simulation Hypothesis and The OA is a topic of popular culture and philosophical inquiry that explores the potential connections between the possibility that our reality is a computer-generated simulation and the television series, The OA.

The OA is a science fiction drama series that follows the story of a young woman named Prairie Johnson, also known as The OA, who resurfaces after being missing for seven years. Prairie recounts her experiences of being held captive and her journey through multiple dimensions, blurring the boundaries between reality and fantasy. The show explores themes of consciousness, identity, and the nature of existence.

The Simulation Hypothesis and The OA are connected through the show's exploration of multiple dimensions and the potential for our reality to be a computer-generated simulation. The show suggests that the characters may exist in different dimensions or simulations, and that their experiences are influenced by these alternate realities.

Moreover, The OA challenges our understanding of the relationship between mind and matter, and the potential for different dimensions or simulations to shape our perception of reality. The show raises questions about the nature of personal identity, the potential for multiple realities to coexist, and the potential for individuals to transcend the limitations of their current existence.

Additionally, The OA raises ethical questions about the potential consequences of manipulating consciousness and the implications of living in a simulated reality. It raises questions about the nature of personal agency, the potential for identity loss or confusion, and the moral implications of creating or controlling simulated experiences.

Overall, the Simulation Hypothesis and The OA are complex and thought-provoking topics that challenge us to question our assumptions about the nature of reality, the potential for alternate dimensions or simulations, and the implications of living in a computer-generated simulation. While The OA is a work of fiction, it offers a thought-provoking exploration of the possibilities of existence and encourages us to contemplate the nature of consciousness and the potential consequences of living in a simulated reality.

CHAPTER 42
The Simulation Hypothesis and The Leftovers

The Simulation Hypothesis and The Leftovers is a topic of popular culture and philosophical inquiry that explores the potential connections between the possibility that our reality is a computer-generated simulation and the television series, The Leftovers.

The Leftovers is a drama series that takes place in a world where a significant portion of the global population mysteriously disappears. The show follows the lives of the remaining individuals as they grapple with grief, faith, and existential questions. It delves into themes of loss, belief systems, and the search for meaning in an unpredictable world.

The Simulation Hypothesis and The Leftovers are connected through the show's exploration of the nature of reality and the potential for alternate interpretations of events. The show suggests that the disappearance of people might be part of a larger plan or a simulation, blurring the boundaries between what is real and what is simulated.

Moreover, The Leftovers challenges our understanding of the relationship between perception and reality, and the potential for reality to be influenced by external forces or simulated experiences. The show raises questions about the nature of personal identity, the search for meaning in a chaotic world, and the human desire to find explanations for inexplicable events.

Additionally, The Leftovers raises ethical and existential questions about the implications of living in a world where reality is uncertain or potentially simulated. It explores the consequences of different belief systems and the impact they have on individuals and society as they navigate grief, loss, and existential crises.

Overall, the Simulation Hypothesis and The Leftovers are thought-provoking topics that challenge us to question our assumptions about the nature of reality, the search for meaning, and the potential consequences of living in a potentially simulated existence. While The Leftovers is a work of fiction, it offers a contemplation of the human experience and encourages us to reflect on the nature of reality and our place within it.

CHAPTER 43
The Simulation Hypothesis and The 100

The Simulation Hypothesis and The 100 is a topic of popular culture and philosophical inquiry that explores the potential connections between the possibility that our reality is a computer-generated simulation and the television series, The 100.

The 100 is a science fiction drama series that takes place in a post-apocalyptic future where a nuclear catastrophe has rendered Earth uninhabitable. The surviving human population resides on a space station called the Ark. When resources on the Ark start to dwindle, a group of young prisoners is sent to Earth to determine if it is habitable. The show explores themes of survival, morality, and the complexities of human nature.

The Simulation Hypothesis and The 100 are connected through the show's exploration of the nature of reality and the potential for our reality to be a computer-generated simulation. The show raises questions about the possibility that the characters' experiences on Earth, the challenges they face, and the conflicts they encounter may be part of a larger simulation or experiment.

Moreover, The 100 challenges our understanding of the relationship between reality and perception, and the potential for our understanding of the world to be shaped or manipulated. The show raises questions about the nature of personal identity, the potential for external forces to influence human behavior, and the moral dilemmas that arise in a complex and unpredictable world.

Additionally, The 100 raises ethical questions about the choices humans make in extreme circumstances, the impact of their actions on others, and the consequences of living in a world where reality may be uncertain or controlled by external forces.

Overall, the Simulation Hypothesis and The 100 are intriguing topics that invite us to contemplate the nature of reality, the complexities of human existence, and the potential consequences of living in a potentially simulated world. While The 100 is a work of fiction, it prompts us to consider the implications of our choices, the limits of our understanding, and the moral challenges that arise in an uncertain and evolving reality.

CHAPTER 44
The Simulation Hypothesis and The Expanse

The Simulation Hypothesis and The Expanse is a topic of popular culture and philosophical inquiry that explores the potential connections between the possibility that our reality is a computer-generated simulation and the science fiction television series, The Expanse.

The Expanse is a futuristic space opera set in a colonized solar system. It follows the interplay between various factions, including Earth, Mars, and the Belters, as they navigate political conflicts, resource scarcity, and the discovery of an ancient alien protomolecule. The show delves into themes of power dynamics, human survival, and the search for meaning in a vast and complex universe.

The Simulation Hypothesis and The Expanse are connected through the show's exploration of the nature of reality and the potential for our existence to be part of a computer-generated simulation. The show hints at the possibility that the events unfolding in the series could be influenced by external forces or manipulated through advanced technology.

Moreover, The Expanse challenges our understanding of the relationship between human agency and the broader forces shaping our reality. The show raises questions about the nature of personal identity, the potential for hidden agendas, and the search for truth within a complex and politically charged universe.

Additionally, The Expanse raises ethical questions about the consequences of our actions, the distribution of power, and the impact of technology on our lives. It explores the ethical dilemmas faced by characters as they confront moral choices in a universe that tests their values and principles.

Overall, the Simulation Hypothesis and The Expanse are captivating topics that encourage us to contemplate the nature of reality, our place within a vast cosmos, and the potential consequences of living in a simulated existence. While The Expanse is a work of fiction, it invites us to reflect on the complexities of human nature, the exploration of space, and the ethical implications of our choices in a future where technology and power dynamics shape our reality.

CHAPTER 45
The Simulation Hypothesis and The Circle

The Simulation Hypothesis and The Circle is a topic of popular culture and philosophical inquiry that explores the potential connections between the possibility that our reality is a computer-generated simulation and the novel and film, The Circle.

The Circle is a dystopian science fiction novel written by Dave Eggers and later adapted into a film. The story follows Mae Holland, a young woman who joins a powerful tech company called The Circle. As she becomes more deeply involved in the company's operations, she begins to question the ethics of its actions, particularly its focus on surveillance and the elimination of privacy. The Circle explores themes of technology, surveillance, and the impact of social media on personal and societal boundaries.

The Simulation Hypothesis and The Circle are connected through the story's exploration of the potential consequences of living in a hyper-connected and heavily monitored world. The novel and film raise questions about the nature of reality, the impact of technology on personal identity, and the potential for our lives to be shaped and controlled by external forces.

Moreover, The Circle challenges our understanding of the relationship between technology and human experience. It raises questions about the nature of personal privacy, the potential for identity loss or confusion in an age of constant surveillance, and the ethical implications of allowing technology to permeate every aspect of our lives.

Additionally, The Circle raises ethical questions about the responsibilities of technology companies and the need for transparency, accountability, and the protection of individual rights. It raises concerns about the potential for power imbalances, the erosion of privacy, and the potential for the misuse of advanced technology.

Overall, the Simulation Hypothesis and The Circle are thought-provoking topics that challenge us to question our assumptions about the nature of reality, the impact of technology on society, and the potential consequences of living in a world where privacy is increasingly compromised. While The Circle is a work of fiction, it serves as a cautionary tale, urging us to critically examine the role of technology in our lives and consider the ethical implications of its pervasive presence in society.

CHAPTER 46
The Simulation Hypothesis and Snow Crash

The Simulation Hypothesis and Snow Crash is a topic of popular culture and philosophical inquiry that explores the potential connections between the possibility that our reality is a computer-generated simulation and the science fiction novel, Snow Crash, written by Neal Stephenson.

Snow Crash is a cyberpunk novel set in a future where corporations hold significant power and people immerse themselves in a virtual reality called the Metaverse. The story follows Hiro Protagonist, a hacker and pizza delivery driver, as he uncovers a conspiracy involving a drug called Snow Crash and a linguistic virus that affects the minds of individuals in both the real world and the virtual realm.

The Simulation Hypothesis and Snow Crash are connected through the novel's exploration of the blurring boundaries between reality and virtual reality. The book suggests that the virtual world of the Metaverse can have profound impacts on the physical world and human consciousness. It raises questions about the nature of reality, the potential for a computer-generated simulation to influence our perception of the world, and the consequences of living in an increasingly immersive virtual environment.

Moreover, Snow Crash challenges our understanding of the relationship between technology, language, and human experience. The book delves into the power of words, the potential for language to shape reality, and the ways in which technology can both empower and control individuals. It raises questions about the potential for identity loss, the commodification of information, and the ethical implications of technological advancements.

Additionally, Snow Crash explores the concept of a hierarchical society governed by powerful corporations, drawing attention to the potential consequences of concentrated power and the influence of technology on social structures.

Overall, the Simulation Hypothesis and Snow Crash are thought-provoking topics that delve into the possibilities and implications of living in a computer-generated simulation and the role of technology in shaping our perception of reality. While Snow Crash is a work of fiction, it invites readers to reflect on the profound impact of technology on society, the boundaries between virtual and physical realms, and the potential consequences of existing in a world where reality and simulation intertwine.

CHAPTER 47

The Simulation Hypothesis and Neuromancer

The Simulation Hypothesis and Neuromancer is a topic of popular culture and philosophical inquiry that explores the potential connections between the possibility that our reality is a computer-generated simulation and the science fiction novel, Neuromancer, written by William Gibson.

Neuromancer is a seminal cyberpunk novel set in a dystopian future where technology and virtual reality dominate society. The story follows a washed-up computer hacker named Case, who is hired for a high-stakes heist that involves infiltrating the powerful artificial intelligence known as Neuromancer. The novel explores themes of artificial intelligence, virtual reality, and the blurring boundaries between the digital and physical worlds.

The Simulation Hypothesis and Neuromancer are connected through the novel's exploration of a world where virtual reality and advanced technology play significant roles in shaping human existence. The book raises questions about the nature of reality, the potential for a computer-generated simulation to influence our perception of the world, and the consequences of living in a world heavily influenced by artificial intelligence.

Moreover, Neuromancer challenges our understanding of the relationship between human consciousness, technology, and the concept of self. The novel delves into the idea of individuals merging their consciousness with virtual reality, blurring the line between physical and digital existence. It raises questions about the nature of personal identity, the potential for identity loss or transformation in a virtual realm, and the ethical implications of manipulating human consciousness.

Additionally, Neuromancer explores the power dynamics between individuals and corporations, drawing attention to the potential consequences of concentrated wealth and the exploitation of technology for personal gain. It also touches on themes of control, surveillance, and the manipulation of information in a world driven by advanced technology.

Overall, the Simulation Hypothesis and Neuromancer are thought-provoking topics that invite us to question the nature of reality, the impact of technology on society, and the potential consequences of living in a world heavily influenced by virtual reality and artificial intelligence. While Neuromancer is a work of fiction, it serves as a captivating exploration of the possibilities and implications of advanced technology on human existence and encourages us to critically reflect on the nature of consciousness and the boundaries between the real and the virtual.

CHAPTER 48
The Simulation Hypothesis and The Singularity

The Simulation Hypothesis and The Singularity are two interconnected topics of popular culture and scientific speculation that explore the potential connections between the possibility that our reality is a computer-generated simulation and the concept of the technological Singularity.

The Simulation Hypothesis suggests that our reality is a computer-generated simulation created by a more advanced civilization or entity. It raises the idea that the universe and everything within it, including our thoughts, perceptions, and experiences, are simulated constructs.

The Singularity, on the other hand, refers to a hypothetical point in the future where technological progress accelerates exponentially, leading to a significant transformation of human civilization. It is often associated with the creation of advanced artificial intelligence (AI) that surpasses human intelligence and leads to radical changes in society and the nature of human existence.

The Simulation Hypothesis and The Singularity are connected through the idea that advanced AI or post-human civilizations may have the capability to create simulations that are indistinguishable from our reality. It is speculated that as technology progresses and approaches the Singularity, the creation of highly realistic and immersive simulations could become possible.

Moreover, both concepts raise questions about the nature of consciousness, the boundaries of reality, and the ethical implications of creating and living in simulated environments. They challenge our understanding of what is real and invite us to contemplate the potential consequences of advanced technology on our perception of reality and the nature of human existence.

The Simulation Hypothesis and The Singularity are complex and intriguing topics that invite philosophical and scientific discussions. While they remain speculative in nature, they stimulate our imagination and push us to explore the limits of human knowledge, the potential directions of technological progress, and the profound implications they may have for our understanding of reality and the future of humanity.

CONCLUSION

Living in a simulated reality, if the Simulation Hypothesis is true, would have profound implications for our understanding of existence and the nature of reality. While the true implications remain speculative, here are some key considerations:

1. Nature of Reality: If our reality is simulated, it would challenge our traditional notions of what is real. It suggests that the world we experience is a carefully constructed simulation, raising questions about the origin, purpose, and ultimate nature of our existence.

   It also poses the question of time itself. Does time really exist?
   Time as we know it is relative and is barely a metric to give us some perception of reality but in effect time is only a conception.

2. Creator and Simulation: The existence of a simulated reality implies the presence of a creator or a higher intelligence capable of constructing and maintaining the simulation.

It raises philosophical and theological questions about the nature of this creator and their motivations.

We know with the string theory that there are an infinite number of dimensions, parallel Universes where an indefinite number of YOU exist.
It is very likely that our Universe is one of many. The big bang which we have used to give ourselves a perception of beginning of time is merely the birth of our Universe and probably the end of another one., adding to the notion that our Universe is part of a multiverse where infinite numbers of Universe exist with its own reality.

3. Consciousness and Identity: If we live in a simulated reality, it would raise questions about the nature of consciousness and personal identity. Are our thoughts and experiences genuine, or are they merely programmed responses within the simulation? It challenges the distinction between real and simulated experiences.

Our reality might just well be an opposite reality from another Universe.
For every thought, action, decision we make, the same opposite reaction would occur in another Universe and the fine structure constant seems to correlate that theory of a perfect harmony throughout the Multiverse.

4. Free Will and Determinism: The concept of free will becomes complex in a simulated reality. If our actions and choices are predetermined by the simulation's programming, it raises questions about the extent to which we have genuine autonomy and the implications for moral responsibility.

    Our actions might not predetermine but the opposite reaction in a parallel Universe.

5. Purpose and Meaning: The existence of a simulated reality prompts us to question the purpose and meaning of our lives. If our experiences are orchestrated within the simulation, it raises the question of whether there is an inherent purpose or if meaning is

subjective and constructed within the
simulation.

6. Ethics and Morality: The ethical implications
   of living in a simulated reality are significant.
   It raises questions about the responsibilities
   of the creator and the potential
   consequences of manipulating
   consciousness within the simulation. It
   challenges our notions of right and wrong
   and calls for ethical considerations in
   creating and operating such simulations.

7. Simulation within Simulation: The possibility
   of nested simulations, where simulated
   realities exist within other simulated realities,
   introduces layers of complexity. It raises the
   question of how far down the simulation
   rabbit hole extends and whether there is an
   ultimate reality beyond simulations.

8. Scientific Inquiry: If we are living in a
   simulated reality, it raises questions about
   the limits of scientific inquiry. Are the laws of
   physics and the rules governing our reality

consistent throughout the simulation, or can they be altered or suspended?

9. Existential Exploration: The idea of living in a simulated reality invites existential exploration and introspection. It challenges us to critically examine our beliefs, perceptions, and assumptions about the nature of reality, consciousness, and the human experience.

10. Implications for Technology: The possibility of a simulated reality has implications for the development and use of advanced technologies. It raises questions about the ethical use of technology, the potential for creating realistic virtual experiences, and the blurring of boundaries between the physical and virtual realms.

Ultimately, the implications of living in a simulated reality depend on the nature and design of the simulation itself. While the Simulation Hypothesis remains speculative, it encourages us to question our assumptions, explore philosophical concepts, and consider the profound implications of the nature of our reality.

"Nothing was, nothing will be; everything is, everything has essence, is present."

Hermann Hesse